FAMILY PORTRAIT

from a Mother's Diary

Anne Marie Zanzucchi

new city press, new york

Published in the United States of America by New City Press,
the Publishing House of the Focolare Movement, Inc.
206 Skillman Avenue, Brooklyn, N.Y. 11211
© 1981 by New City Press, Brooklyn, N.Y.
Translated from the original Italian edition
Giorno per Giorno, Diario di una Mamma by New City Press
Printed in the United States of America
ISBN 0-911782-19-2
Library of Congress Catalog Card Number 81-80031

Contents

Introduction

The following pages are extracts from a mother's daily journal. They reflect the comings and goings, the tensions, crises and joys of one family during the decade of the 70s.

No family could fail to recognize itself in the experiences life offers to Anne Marie Zanzucchi, her husband Dan, and their children. There is the moment when Dan has to undergo serious (possibly fatal) surgery. There are the times when the older children go out into the world to make their own way. There are the observations and worries about a particular child's development—Is my son stealing? What do I do? There are financial worries. There are the joyous times, too—the holidays together, the shared experiences, the happiness of seeing children developing and expressing themselves, making balanced and responsible choices.

5

There are the moments of deep communion between husband and wife.

Life itself is here, as every family knows it, in its bright moments and its dark ones. Yet always, there is something different about this family: a way of loving that puts everything on a different plane.

The life revealed in these intimate pages is a kind of journey into unity, in which each family member expresses himself or herself fully as an individual, while yet being able to live for others. It is a way of life that the parents communicate to their children through their example, in a way that leaves their sons and daughters very free.

In these times of crisis, this book offers a positive contribution to family life.

The Editor

Day by day

March 3, 1970

This has been a very intense day. I was a little tired this afternoon so I lay down on the bed for a while. Shortly after, Frank came home from school. Not finding me in the other rooms, he opened my door with the impetuousness of the seven-year-old that he is.

"Mommy, why are you in bed? Don't you feel well?"

"No, no, I'm okay. Just a little tired."

"You know, Mommy, if you get yourself this tired, maybe you should have had fewer children!"

"You're not the ones who tire me out! Sure, you make work for me. But you also help me. It's this life that we're leading, which is so full, that sometimes makes me a little tired. But it's really nothing. I feel better already. Besides, don't you realize that if your daddy and I had just one less child, you wouldn't be around? You're glad you're here, aren't you? Aren't you glad you're living?"

He stood there thinking for a minute. Then. . . . "Well, sure, I'm glad to be alive. But, you know, it was also a risk!"

At first I thought that Frank was talking about the risk there was for me at the time of his birth. But when I had explained to him a while ago how a child comes into this world, I thought the question was resolved in a simple way. I didn't have the slightest impression that he had been negatively impressed. So I asked him, "In what sense do you mean that it was a risk to bring you into this world?"

"In the sense that things ended up okay, but I could have turned out bad."

I was flabbergasted, but I tried not to show it.

"Well for that matter, all of us can turn out bad at any time. In fact even you can still turn out bad."

"Well. . .there's not much chance of that anymore!"

I didn't continue the conversation. Probably even he would not have been able to explain why he had this conviction.

But it made me wonder. Was it that he felt secure in the environment in which he lived? Could it be that, because we tried to show him with our lives, and, if it was opportune, with our words that God is present and loves us, that he felt secure under the watchful eye of this God of Love?

July 31, 1970
We'll be seeing our children again. They've been travelling around for a month now, to their grand-

parents, to see friends, and the girls have been to a convention for youth.

When school was over we had sort of a round table discussion with all five children to make plans up till August. Each one had said what he or she wanted to do.

On a piece of graph paper, Dan had made a chart in order to get a general idea of where they would all end up, how they would get there, how much the expenses would be (and any expected income).

I once heard that it's not the family that brings up the children, but society. Looking over this chart, I had the distinct impression that, at least for a few months out of the year, the family was not the formative environment, but the world.

We too, Dan and I, had been to a convention—one for married persons.

Now we would be with the children again. I feel a sense of respect for them, in this period in which they were away from us—a time, no doubt, full of experiences both positive and negative, but experiences nonetheless. I don't know what we'll find in them. We'll try to adjust, by loving, by listening.

What Dan and I really need is a rest. We'd love to go off to some secluded place where there's peace and silence. But for now, we can't.

"I have to watch out," I thought to myself during the trip, "not to ruin the vacation for the children by looking for my own—our own— satisfaction."

I'm a little apprehensive about this vacation, at the thought of our children's ages—from seven to sixteen. They'll be coming to me with all their most recent adventures; with their exuberance; with their love of life, of friendships; with some laziness too. While I see myself, at forty, a little worn out.

I could let them all do what they want without worrying about it and without getting involved. But that doesn't seem right. I could get them to do what we want, but this wouldn't be right either. That would be conditioning them. We'll see.

Then too, there are relatives and friends that we'll see once again there, whom we haven't seen for a year. It will be demanding to renew the various relationships.

August 2, 1970

Upon getting up from an afternoon nap, I looked out the window and saw Maryann sitting in the grass reading with great interest a book I had not read. But I knew the author, and I was not sure whether the book would be right for her. I was tempted to go down and say something. But I didn't.

Later she came in with the book.

"Is it interesting?"

"I can't say. I'm still at the beginning."

"I wouldn't mind reading it myself."

"Take this copy. It's Uncle Joe's. I've got Lia's copy too."

In the evening we started discussing the first part of the book together.

August 8, 1970

I finished washing the dishes a little while ago. What a pile! And so many pots and pans! This evening there were ten of us at the table. We were upstairs visiting Grandma and Grandpa. Everybody calls them

Grandma and Grandpa, even we sons and daughters, even other families who live nearby.

All the children were around the dinner table, with Grandpa at the head and Grandma next to him. They were playing cards—all of them! Every so often Grandpa would trick them. Then they'd yell and joke.

I was watching my children and observing their behavior with their grandparents. How different it is from what mine was with them—my parents!—when I was younger. Every so often Michael would jokingly mess up Grandpa's hair. Someone else would start playfully making fun of him. There's a free-flowing relationship there, that they don't even have with us. Maybe it's because their grandparents are free—with respect to them—of any concerns about their upbringing, their formation. Maybe it's because the children perceive that their grandparents, even when asking something of them, are not "commanding" them.

And yet, the children show respect for their grandparents. To some extent they understand their mentality, which is conservative—traditionalist, you could say. Once in a while, they argue with them good-naturedly. But most of the time they don't. They accept their grandparents as they are and get along with them quite easily.

For a long time, Grandpa couldn't accept Michael's long hair, but he goes along with it now.

This mutual respect results in a mutual gift. Grandma and Grandpa experience again some youthfulness; they don't feel forgotten. In fact they feel sought out by their grandchildren, even preferred in a certain respect to us parents.

And the children have certain experiences with

11

their grandparents that they don't have with us. With them, they feel on safe ground. Grandma and Grandpa are always big-hearted and tolerant with them. They never reproach them.

August 10, 1970

"Mommy, I'm taking some money for the bus and for a snack."

"Can't you take a snack with you from home?"

"Yeah, but today I feel like eating a piece of pizza."

"All right. Take what you need from the money that's on the cabinet in the kitchen."

Michael rushed out the door. A little later, I realized that there was more of the money missing in the kitchen than I had anticipated.

At lunch time, Michael came back home. He yelled out, "Hi Mom!" and ran into the living room without even taking off his coat. I waited a moment to be sure I wasn't upset. Then I went to him. There he was on his knees by a table with his album of trading cards, all excited about a pack of trading cards in his hands. "This one I didn't have!" he'd cry out happily. "This one is really hard to get!" He knew I was there, but he didn't lift up his head. Then silence.

"Look at all those trading cards, Michael!"

"They gave them to me," he shot back immediately.

"Is that right? You must have a lot of friends!"

"Well, you know how it is. . . . "

I went back to the kitchen, but I was upset, and I went back to him again. By now my tone of voice had changed.

"You'd better tell me the truth, and I mean it."

"But I told you. They gave them to me."

12

"Michael, you took the money this morning on purpose for the trading cards, and you didn't tell me."

He started mumbling something or other. Then he stopped, and looking away from me continued to fumble around with his things. I made him sit down.

"Listen here. You don't realize the seriousness of what you're doing. You begin with small things—a lie, a little money picked up here and there. Then who knows how you'll end up. And aren't you bothered by the displeasure you cause us and will cause us by going on like this?"

So the sermon went, for a little while longer. Nothing at all was accomplished in that moment. I soon realized my mistake. I spoke to him when I was upset; tore him away from something that interested him enormously; and gave too much importance to the incident.

Later that afternoon, I heard him on the phone with a friend of his, arranging an exchange of one of those famous trading cards—a duplicate. I had settled down by then, and I had spoken to Dan about it. I saw the album on the table and began leafing through it. Michael came back, and I said to him, "You know, these are pretty interesting. And it looks as if you've filled up quite a few pages."

"Yeah, I've got a lot done. Only I'm still missing some that are so hard to get, so hard!"

"Well if you just keep at it, you'll find them—especially if you ask more and more of your friends who are collecting them."

Michael looked at me askance. He seemed to be saying, "What's come over Mommy?"

"Look, Michael, when you feel the urge to buy a

13

whole lot of trading cards, or when you feel you just can't go on without having this or that little card, it's better if you tell me about it. I'll do my very best to get you the money. We'll just skimp on something else. If there's just no way we can afford it, then I'll tell you, and we'll see together what can be done."

Michael looked at me with a gleam of joy in his eyes. Was he seeing all the trading cards he'd be able to get? I don't think so. I had the distinct impression that he was mostly happy over our renewed relationship.

Now that they are getting older, I'll have to see with Dan what we can do. Maybe we can give them a weekly allowance, or make them more accountable, as they grow older, for our economic situation. Maybe we have to do both things at the same time.

September 20, 1970

Lately, Dan has been very taken up with his work, and I too have been immersed in a million projects, all of them very urgent. There hasn't been anything really wrong between us, but neither has there been anything really positive. We've been going ahead day after day burdened by this physical and spiritual tiredness, in the absence of a deeper relationship. The children, especially the smaller ones, have been overactive and particularly mischievous.

Yesterday I said to Dan, "I just can't handle it any more."

It was like opening a carbonated drink that had been shaken up. Everything shot out. It was a rather strong experience. We spoke. We talked for a long time. But we weren't able to really listen to one another. And we ended up harboring judgments toward each other.

Today is Sunday. This morning we decided to go for a ride to a park area we hadn't seen. The weather was glorious. The flowers and fountains should have been enthralling, but I saw that the children weren't interested. One was tired and sat down on a bench. Another just dragged along moaning about this or that. They all would start fighting over the slightest thing. In other words, it was a rather depressing atmosphere.

I got upset. "Listen here, don't you know the first thing about being good?"

I gave the scolding I usually give when things don't go well and which in the end doesn't do a bit of good.

In the evening, as we drove home, there were long periods of silence interspersed with squabbles among the children.

When we got home, Dan and I looked at one another. "This isn't right," we agreed. We were together the whole day (and we seldom have that opportunity) and it seemed instead that we were far away from one another. Everything had gone topsy-turvy. We knew why. The day before, there had been that misunderstanding between us which left its effect not only on us but also on our children. We asked forgiveness of one another in order to re-establish the love between us.

At supper things also changed with the children. We were less tense with them, which at once put us all at ease. They themselves remarked on the difference between our day together and this evening, which found everyone at peace.

October, 1970

I was driving my children along a country road when around a bend there appeared an imposing monastery. I could see a monk reading in a peaceful

15

grotto. Maybe he was praying to God, I thought. Another monk was slowly walking along praying his rosary.

We pulled up to the entrance and went into the church. It was a beautiful church, peaceful and prayerful.

No one else was there except a few monks in prayer.

I knelt down with the children and put myself before God, present there in the tabernacle. But after a few minutes, the children became restless. They began to fuss and move around, so after a quick prayer we left. But within my soul I felt deep regret at not being able to stay with Jesus longer, like those monks.

As we drove down the road, I began to reflect. "Those monks are doing the will of God, which for them means praying many hours each day. Well, the same for me. If I do the will of God, I'm united with him, just as they are."

The thought of Mary came to my mind—Mary, seat of wisdom, yet mother and homemaker. In that instant, I saw my life with all the little things that I have to do in a new light. They were, in part, similar to things she had to do. They were the will of God for me. They were what God in his love offered me in those moments, and I have to respond with love.

My recollection is found in his will. It seemed that the walls of the monastery were thrown open wide. God calls us lay persons to contemplation too.

March 18, 1971

Today is Sunday. The sun was glorious this morning when we woke up. We took the younger ones (the

16

older ones already had plans) for a ride outside the city through the countryside.

As we were leaving the city we passed a church. It was nine and people were going in. We decided to stop for Mass right then. It turned out to be the children's Mass. Near the end, the priest turned to the children and said, "I want you to stay after Mass."

We all left the church. Shortly after (we hadn't even driven away) all the children were already swarming out.

I noticed that Frank had a serious, sulky face.

"What's wrong?" I asked.

"What right did that priest have to keep those children after church?"

"I guess he had something to tell them. And besides, as you saw, he did it quickly. They're already outside playing."

"Okay, but it's still not right for him to keep everyone. What if someone didn't want to stay?"

Dan and I let the subject drop. It didn't seem the right moment to discuss it.

While we were out, though, we talked a little about Frank's reaction. He's the youngest of our children. He's just a little over eight years old, and already he has such a strong sense of freedom—or I should say, such a strong reaction toward those who symbolize authority and impose something.

He doesn't know what true freedom is. He thinks it's doing whatever you want. Instead, true freedom represents a long, difficult conquest, and the capacity for giving, for understanding. It is the capacity to channel one's strength, one's talents, one's energies for the good of oneself and others.

Dan and I are here to help him accomplish this. We have to be careful not to force things on him; yet we have to help him to reason, to understand.

This is a difficult undertaking—to have responsibility for these children yet not abuse our authority.

April, 1971

I had a stressful conversation with my daughter. I listened to her for a long time trying to set aside my judgments of her. I felt like pointing out her mistakes, her erroneous stance, etc.

At the end, I wearily said something, but I was too upset to speak to her calmly. She left.

Being alone, I spontaneously turned to God and "established contact" with him. I prayed without words. I entrusted the girl to him and I understood that she is his daughter and...mine. Every moment had to be newly created from the love that flows between God and me.

June 24, 1971

Michael is taking some very important exams these days. The ones he's finished have gone well, but as for the rest, I get the impression that he's doing nothing to get ready for them.

I've often taken issue with him about this, but I'm not happy with myself for it.

Are these continuous reminders really love, true love, for him, or am I doing it out of some self love, just so he'll do well on this exam? Or are there other reasons?

August 6, 1971

Yesterday there was an especially deep rapport between Dan and me. We were out with all the others, but we were able to go off for a walk on our own. We sat down and talked. We shared many things with one another. In recent times, God has shown us our limits. We've found ourselves almost totally inactive.

Maybe he wants to show us that what counts is not what you do, but how you do it.

The other day when Dan and I were together, I sensed that what counts is to be the first to love. Yet the perfection of love consists in mutual love which is to give of oneself, which is to receive, which is to be received.

August 12, 1971

Now that we're well rested, and with the added incentive of beautiful weather, we've gone on various jaunts with the children.

Splendid locales. Breathtaking views. Strenuous exercise, which I think has done us good. But that certain rapport between Dan and me has suffered a little and what is worse, so has the one with God. We admitted it to one another upon our return this evening.

And we began again.

What a grace it is to be able always to begin again. And to know that in his love God does not make one start all over, but after filling my emptiness he has me continue along the way I've set out upon.

August 20, 1971

Sunday we all went to visit Dr. Rosati, a friend of Dan. The children really looked smart, all combed and dressed up in their Sunday best.

Our vacation together has bolstered our family life by allowing for more leisurely conversation in the absence of normal daily commitments. And because it was lived in an attitude of mutual love, it nourished our unity and better developed each child's personality. So on Sunday you could sense a strong bond among all of us, yet each child appeared different from the rest, each one special in his or her own right.

They made a nice impression on the professor and on his sister. I think I myself was rather proud of them.

Usually, my attitude toward their various gifts is tempered by their faults and limitations. But on Sunday I couldn't see any of them.

A short time later, Frank got sick. Then John got a very high fever. The symptoms were not clearly indicative of a particular illness. What could they have? The doctor said it was a type of virus. Was it serious?

It was an occasion to "straighten out" the way in which I looked upon my children; a reminder to love them for God, to care for them as God's own.

August 23, 1971

In recent days, I've tried to pinpoint the situation with these children of ours—so lively, impetuous and spontaneous as they are. I've wondered if there is a true understanding with them and among them. I knew that we should see all this together. I just had to find the right moment.

Then one day I was on a long train ride with the

three oldest. I asked them some questions. All three of them felt that in their opinion there was a deep accord among all of us, a mutual love that was fairly consistent. But there was also the joking around, the teasing, the "lively" exchanges, the elbowing (and not always just physically). At times they're unkind to one another. In other words, they knew that they could be a little more vigilant.

We spoke about a lot of things. We examined the things that had happened and the areas in which they had grown during the past year, as well as the things that would have to be done.

We spoke about their studies, about true "education," about their investigation of topics or subject matter that interested them, about the "pursuit of knowledge." We talked about the strengthening of the will and the dangers of laziness—one of the products of our consumer society. We discussed decorating their rooms, detachment from things, friendships, and their relationship with God. I would say this was the first time since they've "grown up" that there has been such a deep exchange among us.

August 28, 1971

Looking back on our recent conversation, I understand that with respect to the children and the projects we discussed, I shouldn't push them, nor should I impede them. I just have to "offer," leaving them free.

But if I'm alert to offering perhaps a book, or a suggestion, or a word of caution, while maintaining an attitude of love (while remaining in God, that is) then I'll be offering God through these circumstances. And they won't feel coerced by me, by my way of seeing things. Instead they'll feel attracted by him.

21

March, 1972

We've noticed that one of our boys, the fourteen-year-old, has been seeing a girl fairly regularly. They go for walks. They sit in the park....

He's told us openly that he likes her.

My inclination was to keep close to the situation but not to tell him that he couldn't do this or that. Instead Dan wanted to tell him right out that he was too young for such things and that he should do other things, etc., etc.

So we've been discussing our ideas with one another in order to know what attitude to take.

Today Dan and I were alone in the house with our boy and we brought up the subject. He was well disposed and we were able to talk to him very openly and candidly. He didn't at all try to avoid the subject. He told very simply what he'd been involved in these past months. First he had fallen in love with a certain girl and then had left her because her father didn't want them seeing one another. Now he felt very strongly about this other girl.

Dan and I discussed it with him. We asked certain questions. "Well, what do you think?" "What do you think about the fact that you have a girlfriend at such a young age?" "Is it helpful for the two of you?" "Are these feelings that enrich your personalities?" "Do they overpower you?" "Are you able to converse together, or is it only your feelings that are operating in this relationship?" The questions were posed very calmly, without expectation of clear and all-encompassing answers.

Dan, who as I mentioned, has always believed

"everything in its own good time," came out with expressions that I never would have expected from him. In that moment he seemed like a totally different person. He listened. He immersed himself in the life of this new generation which at times doesn't reason the way we do.

I saw that he mainly tried to pick out the positive aspects of this experience the boy was having, and I realized that this allowed the boy to take note of all the negative points.

July, 1972

The other day, Dan and I took the children to their grandparents' place and then returned home alone. It was a long ride, a good chance for us to talk things over after a very difficult period full of intense activity that didn't allow sufficient time to look into many important matters.

We spoke about the children, for example. Two of them have arrived at a very critical moment in their lives. They have to make some pretty important decisions for their future.

Talking this over, we found that unfortunately we held opposing viewpoints. I wanted to take more into account their inclinations, their deepest aspirations. Dan put much more emphasis on the advantages of professions that offered stability and security. This in itself wasn't so bad. The trouble was that we each held rigidly to our positions. In fact, it seemed to me that the viewpoints from which we each looked upon their particular problems stemmed from totally opposite views of life. This took me quite by surprise, after so many years of marriage.

We changed the subject. Still, no matter what subject we confronted, whether it related to decisions that had to be made or expenses to plan for or plans to be made, the same thing happened: we held opposing positions.

We resigned ourselves to a halt in the discussions.

In the awkward silence that followed, I asked myself a lot of questions. "How did we ever come to this point when we care so much about one another? Is it because, despite our common choice of a Christian life, we're basically different? Is this the lack of communication that psychologists and sociologists speak about so much in our times?"

The fact is that there seemed to be an abyss between Dan and me, with no chance of our coming together. It was acutely painful to feel, after so many years of marriage, that I was facing a stranger. Even the heat in the car began to close in on us, as in a vise, and seemed to be suffocating us.

We decided to stop for a while.

We parked the car and walked into a field. The shade of the trees was refreshing. I began to turn things over in my mind.

What had happened? Then it struck me. The answers came sharp and clear. "You want to impose your thinking because you're sure that you're right. You pretend to listen to Dan, but you really aren't. You don't give him the slightest edge. You expect everything from him. You don't try in the least to understand his thinking. Is this how you've chosen to relate to others, and in particular, to your husband?"

24

Meanwhile, I glanced at Dan and saw that he was very pensive. I got the impression that he was thinking the same thoughts.

We got back into the car. Little by little—I'm not sure which one of us took the initiative—we started talking again. At first, Dan was disheartened. He went back to his childhood, to his education, to the way his personality had been formed, to his mentality and his defects.

"I'll never be able to change; no matter what I do— and I've tried a lot of things—I'll always be the same."

He felt powerless before himself. I too experienced and admitted the same helplessness, the same awareness of my limitations.

While we listened to one another, with a sense of pain but careful to perceive and receive the very essence of one another, the wall that had risen up between us began to fall. We felt we were understanding one another, and we discovered distant causes of our way of being, the circumstances that had molded us. We took an enormous step ahead in our knowledge of one another.

We arrived at a clear insight. We always knew that our love is rooted in, nourished on, and continuously renewed by nothing other than the relationship that each of us has with God. This love makes up for what's missing, covers over our defects and breaks through our conditional responses.

We were now able to approach the subjects that before seemed to divide us. And in our efforts to understand one another's motives, we were able to distinguish what was right and true. Unforeseen solutions came out that satisfied both of us. Or in some cases, we good-naturedly accepted the fact that we could not resolve certain particular problems at that time and would have to patiently wait for things to work themselves out more.

September 20, 1972

I came home on the bus today with my daughter who is just sixteen. She had been over to her cousin's and I had been to see my mother. We met at our common connection and sat waiting together for the bus.

I saw that she was rather solemn, so I started making conversation. "How was your visit?" "Was it nice?" "Did you have fun?" She answered in monosyllables. "Yes." "No." "I don't know." So I began to tell her about my visit.

All of a sudden she interrupted me. "I have something to tell you. I met a boy and I think I like him."

I tried not to react, not by being insensitive, but by showing neither approval nor disapproval. I tried to be disposed only to listen to what she had to say to me, and also to help her express herself if she wanted that.

She began, with some difficulty, to tell of her dilemma. She felt she cared a lot for this boy. (He was quite young, as, for that matter, was she.) But she had doubts because he wasn't of our faith and even more so, because he did not hold certain values that were fundamental for her. She communicated to me the upheaval caused in her by these affections being accompanied by this perplexity.

I said nothing. I tried with all my strength to parti-

26

cipate in—practically to relive, through what she told me or didn't tell me—all that she had been going through.

October 15, 1972

Sometimes in the afternoon, when my daughter returns from school, I stop by her room. Every so often, I ask how she's feeling. But if I see that it's not the right moment, I don't say anything. I've already told everything to Dan.

I try to keep alive a dialogue with her, but without pushing her. This is so that if she wants to say something to me, she'll feel comfortable doing so.

November 30, 1972

Today I noticed that while she was studying she began to cry. So I said to her, "This thing is really hurting, isn't it?"

"How wouldn't it? I'm going to see him tomorrow, and I don't know what to do."

I kept silent. I knew that only she could bring herself to a decision.

In the evening I stayed with her a long time, till very late at night. I tried to understand. I wanted her to be able to express herself, to get it into the open, even if confusedly, all her doubts and all the love she felt for this boy.

After these hours spent together, in a shared suffering, she came to her conclusion.

"No, I can't go on. Maybe I could make a difference for him because if he doesn't have me maybe he'll hit the skids the way he did before I was around. But I just

27

can't. Something inside me tells me that I can't commit my life and my love like this when I'm feeling this uncertainty inside."

December 4, 1972

My daughter communicated her decision to him the other day when she saw him, with more courage and firmness than I would ever have expected. No matter what he said as he tried not to lose her, there was no turning back for her.

The two of us have had a beautiful relationship these past days. She suffers for having broken this bond of love with this boy, but she's at peace.

I asked her, "Can I do anything?"

"No," was her response, "I know what I did was right so I have to be strong. I have to remain firm in my decision, no matter how much it hurts."

Martha

January, 1973

This morning, Martha moved into our house with her one-week-old baby, Paul. Dan and I had gone to pick her up from the maternity ward of the hospital while the children had stayed home and made the final preparations to welcome our new guests.

We met Martha through a friend of ours. She's not exactly a young woman, and she's courageously faced her maternity alone. She has an uncertain future. The next step is to help her find a job and a place to live, or to situate her and the child with her own family.

Right now, Martha doesn't see how the latter solution could be possible. She doesn't know. She feels a lot of hesitation and uncertainty. We were asked, very discreetly, by this friend of ours if we could take Martha in for a while, maybe a few months, until she was able to make other arrangements.

29

When this proposal was made to us, Dan and I tried thoroughly to evaluate the situation, with all the negative ramifications it contained, especially with respect to the children. We weren't worried about restricting ourselves a little in order to give Martha space to move about with a certain amount of freedom. She was a person in trouble and it was logical to make some sacrifices for her. Also for the children, this would be no great difficulty. What worried us most was that our family intimacy might be affected. Moreover, the presence of a person whose way of life was different from ours could have negative effects on our children. They might figure, for example, that we condone a certain type of relationship between a man and a woman even outside of matrimony.

We talked it over between us. Then, after reassuring each other that we would communicate every eventuality and that we would always be very observant, we decided to speak about it to the children.

They thought the thing was possible so we all agreed to take in Martha and her child.

Now they're here with us. For the moment it's a little awkward for both her and us, but we're hoping that will change.

February, 1973

It's a month now, and, despite all the difficulties, I'm beginning to feel that an open, uncomplicated relationship is possible with Martha. Every so often we have a good long conversation together. We've talked a lot about the past, and I've begun to know of or intuit many of her sufferings.

We still can't see any possibilities for the future, despite our inquiries and efforts. But I'm confident. We'll try to be confident together.

The child is beautiful. The children fuss over him a lot, maybe a bit too much. The little one has undoubtedly given our house an air of excitement.

At suppertime when we're all around the table, Paul's cradle is near Michael, who sits at the head of the table. With a fatherly air, Michael rocks the baby and gives him his pacifier if he whimpers a little.

The insertion of both mother and child into our family has been accomplished. We lead our lives pretty much as before, and even our family relationship has up till now not been affected.

March 15, 1973

These past few days, I've noticed one or another of my children every so often looking intently at the baby. I see a seriousness in their faces, and sometimes a touch of sadness.

This evening, Martha went to dinner at the home of a woman who is a friend of hers. So at suppertime, we were able to talk freely with the children about the situation and hear a little of how they saw things.

Michael began. "You know, Martha and Paul being in our house really makes me think. Lots of times, the attitude of boys toward girls is very superficial. I'm more aware of that now than before. They only see the physical aspect or relate just with their feelings. They don't realize that the love between a man and a woman is something really serious. And marriage too. I'm starting to look at it in a different way. Actually, I always did think of it as something important, because it gave me, through you, the possibility of having a stable family and a sense of security. But up till now, none of this has made an important difference in my way of viewing the question of boy-girl relationships. I knew that relations between a man and a woman before and outside marriage were not a good thing. But I'm not sure if I was entirely convinced.

"Now, when I look at this child without a father and with a mother who's worried and tense about her shaky situation, I can see how much men often take things lightly and act irresponsibly. It hurts me so much to see this baby, that I would do just about anything so that he wouldn't have this emptiness ahead of him."

All this got us into a very extensive and deep conversation on the subject.

At one point, Dan interrupted and asked, "Tell me, did the fact that we took in this girl ever make you think that we might to some degree go along with a certain type of relationship that is nowadays considered very normal by many people?"

"Absolutely not," Clare insisted. "We're quite aware that the wrongs people might for various reasons commit, and the help one gives to those who have to face up to the consequences of their behavior, are two different things. And besides, I really think that Martha has understood a lot of things, don't you?"

May, 1973

A lot of things have happened in these past months. Martha now seems to be convinced that it's better to return to her own family.

I'm going to try to stay near her as much as possible in this period so that she'll have the strength to deal with her family and especially with the attitudes of the people in her neighborhood, who still don't know anything about her situation. But the bond between her and the baby is so strong that it will be one of the best aids in helping her to overcome the difficulties she's sure to face.

Moreover, she's re-established a relationship with God (which for that matter she never really lost completely). This is what will really sustain her.

June, 1973

During her months with us, Martha has noticed things that we have never made too much of, because in our relationship with our children we're more inclined to act according to what seems best in the present moment.

Today she said to me, "You really have a nice family! Each one has his or her own life, with special interests, different hobbies. Each one goes along his or her own way, and yet, I've hardly ever seen a family so united. You and Dan have been able to allow your children freedom of expression, even though it has cost you some peace and tranquility as well as that static kind of order you find in many families. The children are able to communicate with you and with one another. And they're so different from one another that if you had given them the slightest bit of pressure in the wrong way, you would have squelched them—or at least they wouldn't have turned out the way they did."

At this point, she cited some examples: Maryann,

with her "art," and her room, which is a cross between an artist's studio and a shopping gallery; Michael with his music (modern music, of course), which pierces our eardrums from morning to evening; John with all his sports—accompanied by mud, sweat, and all his paraphernalia.

A while back, Dan and I were talking about this and we realized that almost without being aware of it, we really have tried to be receptive to all the inclinations of each one of them through the years. And, as much as possible (within the confines of our rather calculated economic situation as well) we have done what we could to help these sometimes rather hidden gifts come to the surface and be expressed.

And besides, we've seen that in developing these qualities, the children strike a much better balance among themselves because none of them can really feel "superior" to or "better" than the others. One excels in one area. Others excel in other areas. One does exceptionally well in school but can't change a light bulb without breaking it. Another labors and trudges through the books but can do electrical wiring with ease or fix a broken lock, etc.

Moreover, this diversity of gifts, capabilities and interests has enabled them to have contacts with many people of the most varied types. This has helped them a lot in opening up toward others.

Concerning the harmony and unity among all of us that impressed Martha, I think it's due to that degree of respect, mutual love, and "mercy" that we've tried to have toward one another.

A gift anew to one another

May 5, 1974

We're both in the hospital, Dan on the floor below. It's test after test. I let the doctors examine me thoroughly.

Why don't I do the same thing with my soul? Why don't I let God "examine" me and abandon myself totally to him instead of holding back, keeping some things to myself, making small and large compromises?

Sometimes the tests are bothersome and painful, but I feel I should cooperate just the same, I should help, and not tense up. After all, it's for my own good.

This is how I have to be with God. He wants to work in me for my good. I have to cooperate with what he is doing, which is sometimes painful. I can't withdraw from the suffering, which very often is the only means for uniting ourselves with him and with one another.

May 6, 1974

Today we received some very good news regarding someone we care very much about and are very indebted to. Dan and I were filled with a great joy over this news.

Shortly after this, our doctor told me that an X-ray examination revealed the possibility that Dan might be seriously ill. A future examination was necessary, which involved some risk. He left us free to decide whether to undergo it or take other treatment.

I was stunned. Dan, instead, took it calmly. We decided in favor of the examination. The best thing is to prepare ourselves for whatever God wants, with the certainty that it's all his love.

I am not able to sleep. A sense of desperation seems to be welling up inside me. But just as it seems to overwhelm me, I get the strength to say my "yes" to God.

I'm experiencing two things within me. One is suffering, which stems from my affection, my love for Dan. I feel part of myself being ripped away, so strong is this reality of being "one flesh," of being everything that is of Dan. The other is something that almost dominates the suffering. It's the knowledge, the understanding that God is the love that encompasses everything.

He is the Doctor who guides the hands and minds of doctors. He is the Father of our children, who will keep Dan with them as long as he thinks necessary. He is the Friend who is near us in this time of suffering.

If it's what he wants, he can work the miracle—the miracle of keeping Dan with us, or the miracle—if the moment of "separation" has come—of keeping us united just the same.

May 7, 1974

This morning at seven o'clock Mass, we offered everything to Jesus.

Deep within me, I feel very peaceful, but the trouble is that I keep crying. In any case, we're able to talk together, to share our thoughts. I feel that Dan is courageously facing the prospect that the operation will not go well, that he could even die on the operating table. There is a very slim chance of this, but it can happen.

At one point, he told me that he wanted to make a will. We thought over our situation a little, but we had no possessions to dispose of so we dropped the subject.

I left his room. It's clear to both of us that this trial is putting us in front of God. It's as if Jesus, who first united us, is putting himself between us to separate us.

I went back in the afternoon and found Dan making a picture of a little rustic house for his roommate. He's very much at peace. He said to me, "After you left this morning, I lay in bed thinking. Who knows what God wants? I got this desire to live every day from now till Monday as if my life was going to end then. I can't do anything extraordinary, but I feel every action can become 'solemn.' It may seem strange to you, but a deep peace has come over me."

May 8, 1974

I have been discharged from the hospital. We

decided together that it was better for me to return home until Monday. There are a few more days before the operation, and it's best to look in on the children.

I didn't want to leave Dan. He gave me a long letter for the children (spanning more than a year) with lots of drawings in it about life in the hospital. It was both serious and humorous. He portrays himself as allergic to needles and other hospital implements. Then he shows himself overcoming all this by sharing in the lives, the pains, and the joys of others on his floor.

Returning home, I felt "alone." Maybe Dan would no longer be at my side in the future. I found myself beginning to act differently from before, as if I could no longer lean on him. I can't explain it, but I felt I now had to make every decision alone. I had to face the children alone.

I got home, said "hello" to everybody, and with a composure that I couldn't account for, told them about their Dad's situation. They understood the seriousness of his condition. We agreed to say "yes" together to whatever God wanted.

After that, they told me what had been going on in my absence. The atmosphere was the usual one—lively, busy, at times playful. But deep down, there was a clear understanding of what really mattered, an awareness that life is only a "passing through."

Now, as I write, a thought comes to mind: this sense of "aloneness" which lasted throughout the day makes me think of those persons who consecrate themselves to God in the single life. They espouse God, and, yes, this does result in a deep, exclusive relationship with him. But it is one built on an "aloneness." Today, I understood them better.

May 10, 1974

I bought some shoes for John, did the shopping for the week, and made sure Clare knew all the things she had to watch around the house. In the afternoon, I had private conversations with Michael, with Clare, and with Maryann. Simple conversations. Sincere ones.

May 13, 1974

I was in church while Dan was on the operating table. I prayed without words. I was in the presence of God. Various phrases turned over in my mind. "Your faith has saved you. Go in peace." "If your faith were as large as a mustard seed, you could say to this mountain, move, and it would move." "If you had not doubted in your heart...." "Whatever you ask of the Father in my name, I will grant it to you."

I asked Jesus, present in that church, for Dan's full recovery.

May 20, 1974

Dan has been discharged from the hospital. We're now in a tiny house put at our disposal by a friend for the period of convalescence. The operation went well. There was nothing seriously wrong. He has to take care of himself and go for regular checkups.

In the peacefulness of this sort of hermitage, I am very much aware that the love of God has given us back to one another. Dan is a new gift of God for me and I am a new gift of God for Dan.

The love we have for one another is much greater than before.

Vacation, 1974...or, life in community

August 7, 1974

I'm staying close by Dan's side this vacation. Today, while I followed along with him looking here and there for a good place to paint a picture, I felt that our vacation was an opportunity for me to show my love for him.

Usually, a person thinks of a vacation as a time to do whatever he or she pleases. But it's no longer that way for us. It is the love between us that has to guide and make our vacation. Only in this way will it be real.

August 8, 1974

Sometimes I still get fearful about the future. But how can I have fear of a God who only "can" love? My children certainly don't fear me. And I'm only human. How can I possibly feel fear instead of the love of God?

August 9, 1974

Today was, to all appearances, a quiet one. But within me there was a lot going on. This evening I felt I had lost my joy, yet at the same time, my soul was close to God—to his will in that moment, to his love, which goes beyond circumstances that may not always be the best (because of Dan's health and other matters).

August 10, 1974

We're getting into the swing of vacation life here among our relatives and friends. Being in the midst of so many persons, each one a fascinating world unto himself or herself, there's the danger of getting taken up in a life "outside." Instead, I feel that no matter what's happening outside, I have to always "live within."

Every so often when I'm alone—such as this morning searching for mushrooms in the woods, or before taking an afternoon nap, or on other occasions—I get a sense of redirection; there's a rediscovery of life's meaning, of the right way of life.

After looking for mushrooms, the opportunity arose to be with a few of the older girls. Immediately, there was a sharing of experiences, of thoughts.

Today, we gathered all the younger children together, ours and our nieces and nephews. There are thirteen in all, from four to eleven years old. We wanted to alert them to certain things and suggest standards by which we could be of mutual help to one another. Otherwise there might be a lack of concern for one another. They really got involved and were very interested. Afterwards, however, some of them had certain reactions to it all.

It's very demanding to interact with the little ones. I think that those most able to help them are really the older children. Even if we don't intend to, we at times impose our ideas or our way of thinking. Also, we always convey that certain air of authority.

August 12, 1974

Clare and Michael arrived from one of the Mariapolis gatherings*. They're very tired but full of life. You can really sense their input!

Life in our vacation community is very intense; it's full of variety and the unexpected!

Today I was tired; I felt as if I was going to collapse. It seems useless trying to get some rest in these circumstances. Maybe it was a mistake to plan our vacation in this way. I don't know. One thing is certain, though. In every present moment, there is the possibility of believing in God's love.

August 13, 1974

Yesterday evening, Dan and I were together with our four oldest children. We spoke about the Mariapolis, about their friendships, about this vacation. Little by little, the conversation got more serious. We began

---

*Summer gatherings of the Focolare Movement, which involve talks on spiritual themes and exchanging experiences. They are held in many countries around the world.

talking of their possible future choices, about marriage. It was a simple, peaceful and deep exchange.

When we were alone, Dan and I continued the conversation of yesterday with the children. We looked back over our twenty-one years of marriage. They have been very intense and very "full" years. What accounted for the enrichment of our life together? We concluded that it must have been the ongoing effort to maintain mutual love, which resulted in the presence of Jesus, as he himself promised to those who are united in his name.

Moreover, we've always felt that only in this way would our union be truly formative with respect to our children. They'd be more attracted by Jesus present in our midst and choose him, "the most beautiful of the sons of men," rather than the mere idea of marriage— whether or not they were meant to marry. Then, for him, they would follow along the way he had planned for them.

August 14, 1974

Yesterday, I went on a nice outing with my brother and twelve boys from twenty-three years of age on down. It was a spendid day from dawn to dusk. The mountain scenery was magnificent. There was peace among all. No one insisted on his own way. Everyone tried to do what seemed best for the whole group.

In the evening on the way back, we stopped for Mass. I was still envisioning the peaks, the sun, the blue sky. I felt attracted to Jesus, to this Person who made me understand that everything I saw was a reflection of his love, that he is love, that he loves me.

I'm glad that each evening at seven, we always

43

have our appointment with Jesus at Mass. Of course, this puts limitations on our outings. We have to get back on time, and we can't always do what we'd like to.

August 15, 1974

Dan didn't come with us today on our outing. I felt something was different, but I didn't stop to think about it. I realized what it was when we met up again. Normally, when I'm with Dan, I automatically check out my ideas, my thoughts, with his. At times we do this verbally; at times without words. And Dan does the same. This is so enriching for us and so enriching for our relationship!

This evening, at supper, we had a very serious conversation with Michael and Clare, one that resulted in a commitment, you could say. You'd get the impression that we were talking to adults; and yet, they're actually still youths. I understood that maturity, true maturity, is Jesus within a person.

August 17, 1974

Yesterday we went on a long outing. When we returned, I asked myself, "Did I live for myself or for God?" I felt that I was able to answer that by now we've acquired a certain attitude when we're with the others. It's become almost "natural" to live, not for ourselves, but for them.

I feel it is this true love that must increase, the love that makes us understand that to love those around us is to love God. And those around us must feel from our love, from our presence, the love of God.

August 20, 1974

What a hard day this has been! And it's not that we didn't have a lot of rest and relaxation. I found myself with empty hands, so to speak, this evening. I felt a certain discomfort; a sense of dissatisfaction. I saw that the most dangerous moments, so to speak, are those spent in relaxation when adults start talking among themselves. It's not always the case, but very often you can end up in conversation that's superficial, self-serving, purposeless.

What I ended up with was a feeling of uselessness, not of rest.

I resolved to remember more often when I found myself in such situations, that God is love and that I have to be love for those I'm with. Then I would also be rested.

August 22, 1974

The other day, upon returning to the house with Dan after a walk together, we found a rather tense atmosphere. The younger children had been up to all kinds of mischief and the older ones hadn't been able to control things.

We decided to gather everyone together and hear them out. The dining room was full of boys and girls. Beginning with the smallest ones, the six-year-olds, they all had a chance to tell their own version of the facts and events. Without being aware of it, they gave healthy, constructive criticism for themselves and for others. At the end, everyone felt new. No one had bad feelings. Instead, each felt he or she had participated in the good and the bad of all there.

"Peter really did start it all," concluded the littlest one there, "but we all did wrong after that."

Among other things, the whole event was as funny as could be due to the different expressions, the mannerisms, the simplicity with which they told their side of things. But they took it so seriously that no one ever laughed.

It was, I think, a lesson for the smaller ones. They learned to listen to one another, to know one another, to look more deeply into things, and to forgive.

One of my little nephews said at the end, "You know, Aunt Anne, we have to do this more often. Maybe not too long; otherwise we'll get tired of it, but more often because lots of times we need to speak to one another and tell each other what we think."

I think it was also a lesson for the older ones. At one point, one of the little ones said that for them, certain kinds of joking around aren't allowed, but the older ones can do anything they want. "They think they're kings."

My answer was that even the older ones can be in the wrong, especially when they do things just to please themselves instead of for the good of all concerned. Still, I tried to explain the reasons they acted in such and such a way on this or that occasion.

There was a deep soberness among all the little ones. Maybe it was the first time they felt themselves equals, because we were all searching together, with the desire only to help one another be better.

Today we planned an outing. It was a difficult undertaking to involve thirty people ranging from seventy-seven (Grandpa) to four (Luke), as well as mothers expecting babies. We ended up deciding to go for a hike in the countryside, with a longer and more vigorous walk planned for the more hearty souls. But after we started out, a hitch in the plans erupted into bad feelings. An agreement couldn't be reached and it turned out that everything was held up.

Usually I take things in hand in such situations and try to resolve them. But today I didn't make a move. I waited. I was unsure about forcing myself on the situation. Also, I felt that everyone had to make the effort to overcome himself or herself to reach consensus with the others.

August 24, 1974

Yesterday we went out looking for a house to rent for next year. In the process, we were presented with the opportunity—if we joined in with our brothers and sisters—of buying a small, old house that would gradually have to be fixed up.

I talked it over with Dan while we were returning. If circumstances bring us in this direction, we'll do it. But nothing can really add to or take from us. The important thing is to watch how things develop with love and detachment.

August 26, 1974

Vacations are coming to an end. Even the weather is starting to change. It's raining all the time. A few of the children weren't feeling well. Maybe there's a bit of flu going around.

I'm convinced that whatever the moment we find

ourselves in, it contains a beauty all its own—the love of God. It's up to me, to us, to discover it.

So what does it matter if it's vacation or work or being well or not so well? It's all so secondary. It's all a means of receiving the love of God and returning to him—if you can say so—a little love.

Often, in the mornings, Dan and I have been able to talk leisurely with one another. There's been a simple exchange of thoughts, ideas, and experiences. We've gone effortlessly from one subject to another. We've spoken of our relationship with God, of our children, of political and social topics. We've spoken about us, about our love and about our mistakes. . . .

In such moments, there doesn't exist the "secular" and the "sacred." Everything takes on an air of the "sacred."

I feel that this time of vacation has enabled us to open our souls completely to one another, without reservations, without compromise, without excuses. Such a communion, however, is a very delicate thing. It requires a great attentiveness, an availability, a perceptiveness.

August 28, 1974

Yesterday there was a lot of interior peacefulness despite all the pain. There was opportunity for conversation, for a deep rapport with young and old.

In the evening, my brother-in-law showed films from previous vacations.

The children really had a lot of fun seeing segments out of their lives and how much they changed and grew up.

For us too, it was really nice to see scenes from our lives in a family atmosphere that might be termed, "patriarchal," considering the many families present, the elderly, the youths, the babies.

It's a rather atypical partriarchal family, though. Because everyone enjoys such freedom of expression, of movement (within limits of respect and mutual understanding, however), you'd be more inclined to call it a community than a patriarchal family. We've felt that up till now vacation in this manner has been helpful for our children as well. It has led them to take the little ones more into account, to take part in the various tasks for the good of everybody, to share in the lives and problems of other young people, to be aware of the experiences, the sincere efforts, the sacrifices of the adults. In other words, it has been an experience of loving.

Community life frees us from a lot of rigid molds. Moreover, it helps us to develop properly, because, if we really follow this path, it teaches us to be the first to love. However, in my opinion, community life is really what it should be only when there's authentic Christian life behind it. Otherwise it can become group selfishness or still worse, an exploitation of others for one's own personal gain.

August 31, 1974

The other evening we ate out with the older children. We went for pizza. It was a chance to get away without having the little ones around.

There was a very relaxed atmosphere, but—can you believe it?—we couldn't keep things light with

49

these young people. Right away, they wanted to get into serious matters.

First they told us how they viewed their parents' relationship and the influence this relationship had on them and on the whole family. Then they spoke about marriage in general and what was behind the husband-wife relationship.

Finally, they went on to talk about the life of the Church today, about obedience to the Church and the different problems and opinions that ensue from this.

There was no controversy involved in the conversation; only sincerity and openness. We didn't draw conclusions. The only conclusion was that of understanding how to dialogue, how to listen, how even to "lose" one's own ideas in order to understand the others. In other words, there was an understanding of how a person must love even in those instances when he or she perhaps might not want to give in for fear of losing out.

Yesterday morning, we had a constructive conversation. My sister, one of our brothers, and my mother (we "grownups," in other words) were present.

Vacationing together had enabled us to get to know better, not only our own children, but also our nieces and nephews. We had the chance to see them interact among themselves and with others.

Both the positive and the negative came into relief. The negative things saddened us a little and almost seemed to cloud over the good effects of this time spent together.

In the afternoon, we again found ourselves together. We sat on the grass in front of the house. Everyone still felt a little of the disappointment from the morning, but little by little we all got over it. Each of us tried to value fully what the others were saying, their thoughts and their opinions.

The positive side of our children was highlighted and appreciated out of a sincere effort to love, not because of egoism or a natural sense of pride. The negative aspects, or better, the limitations of our children were faced squarely and realistically. And actually, we saw that a better knowlege of these shortcomings prompted us to want to help them more and help each other more too.

September 1, 1974

While saying my prayers, I had to stop at a certain point and examine myself: "Something's not right within me. I belong to God. How does he see me in this moment of my life?"

I felt that in that very moment, God was with me, that he loved me and had given me that "darkness" as a gift. He wanted to tell me something. I opened myself to his love, welcoming the suffering that came from the little bit of confusion I had within.

September 2, 1974

Christina had given a book to Clare. For no particular reason, I picked it up while they were playing catch close by. I read some of the introduction and leafed through it.

It seemed weighty to me. Clare wasn't mature enough to understand the deeper meaning behind it or to distinguish its merits from its limitations. She could possibly get sidetracked by the more spicy parts, thereby distorting the true meaning of the book.

I decided I would read it and then we'd talk about it together.

I read it in the afternoon. Every so often I was tempted to drop it, but I kept on for their sake, in order to maintain their trust, and keep open the lines of communication. In the midst of all its faults, I actually found some very beautiful human values. And its limitations seemed to accentuate the beauty of Christianity.

At supper, there was a spirited exchange, which in the end was very constructive for everyone.

Reflections and other things

November, 1974

With all the talk about abortion, I often find myself going back to those very precious moments of my life when I was expecting my children.

Of all the many arguments in favor of abortion, I have always been dumbfounded and repulsed by the hypothesis, accepted by a few theologians too, that the fruit of conception is not, at least for the first few weeks, a human being. My whole being rebels at this claim.

I remember how much the first moment I had certainty there was a new person within me always meant to me. Knowing the value of every human being, this fact always caused me joy and wonder. It moved me and made me grateful for what nature, for what God himself through his laws, wondrously brought about. I was aware that a new "presence" had entered my life—

and into my relations with others—one that would last forever. With the passing months, the prenatal development, the birth, the growth of the child after it came into the world, all served to deepen that relationship with "another," distinct from me, which had been established from the time of conception.

I find it impossible to believe that for a few weeks, there was only beingless matter in me, not a life, but a kind of appendage that I could dispose of as something that was my own. For me it's absurd to think there could be a "gap" between the moment of fertilization and the moment in which a person begins to exist. It's like segmenting two integrally united realities; that is, conjugal love and the fruit of conception. It's like severing the tree from its roots.

Besides, scientists state that from the moment of conception, "that person," "that" one and no one else, is developing according to a particular "formula." This makes sense to me. I remember how from the very first moments, I always loved my baby with a personal singular love. I loved "that" baby, not another.

I know that what I'm saying could at least in part be due to my emotions and feelings. Still, over the years I've seen that my experience in this area has been similar—very similar—to that of other mothers. Sure, it's true. Affections, feelings, emotions, certainly play a part. But these too are components of "being a woman." They are chords that vibrate, not for nothing, but because of a profound reality that follows the order of the things of God—the reality of motherhood.

Someone could also say that I have lived and experienced these things because I am a believer. Indeed, the Christian ideal has enabled me to live my maternity with fulness. But I really don't think the way I feel is that different from all the other women of the world.

I think we have to help one another to better understand the value of life, of maternity and fatherhood. Otherwise, we'll end up making people, especially young people, more and more irresponsible about their actions.

I'm the first to agree that we all have the duty to eliminate the social causes that lead many women to have an abortion. But you still can't distort the truth, which is spelled out in the consciences of people when it is not obscured by selfishness.

December 30, 1974

Balance sheets and budgets all afternoon. It was fairly easy to assess the year just ending, but planning a new budget has been very complex. Our income is what it is. But the cost of living keeps going up. And the needs of the children are always increasing. We have been trying to break even, but no matter how we try to cut spending, we're always behind. I feel we're doing everything possible to cut corners. We buy in volume. We limit our clothing purchases. We try to take good care of things so they last longer. We use the car only when necessary.

Maybe we could eliminate our summer vacations, but this wouldn't solve anything. We pay very little for our accommodations, and our expenses are the same as they are at home. And besides, we feel that these vacations are very helpful for our family and a significant period in the upbringing of our children.

So what could we do? We agreed that we shouldn't

blow this out of proportion. We decided to communicate the situation to our children and see what they thought.

So...a general assembly was called. As soon as the order of the day was established, Frank asked, "Mommy, we're going bankrupt, aren't we?" And he smiled as if he were pulling my leg, because this was the expression that I sometimes used on him when he would ask me for money for his own things.

Dan explained everything to them. We looked over our income and our expenses for the year ending; the forecast....

The children at once chimed in. "You can't work any more than you are, so it looks like we'll have to do something." They had helped a bit during the past year—but it wasn't much. So together we looked into the various possibilities. Clare is working for her M.A. She could get more secretarial and typing work and also try to do some substitute teaching.

Maryann could make more on her "artistic" productions. (For her, it's something of a suffering to sell the things she does because they're a little like her own children.) We cautioned her, however, not to let her work be determined by the economic situation. For example, it certainly wouldn't be good for her to do the same thing over and over because it sells well.

Mike is finishing his second year of college. He's made a little money with his music. Maybe he could make more. Also, he sometimes gets a job unloading trucks.

So the conclusions were that we have to work more; we have to be more careful with our spending; we have to be ready to do without vacations or other things if necessary—all this without letting the problem become an obsession and lead to miserliness.

But the most important thing came to light at the end. We have to remember (after having done our part) that it is written, "Ask and it will be given to you."

March 18, 1975

There was an assembly at Frank's school. I was there as a representative of the parents. All the teachers were there, and, counting me, four parents. It was very interesting.

These gatherings could be of some importance for the education of our children. I say, "could," because, as of yet, they aren't.

Today I got to know the various teachers better, with their talents and limitations. Some have a strong desire to do good, to build something. The combined efforts of teachers, students and parents could produce much, much more if everyone were committed to work at it, to collaborate. Even so, things are starting to move.

When there are a lot of us together in the general meetings, each one with his or her own ideas to get across, things get pretty unruly. We can be so incapable of listening, of understanding. Sometimes the ensuing chaos is unbelievable. Also, the obstacles, which stem from many prejudices, are evident.

In these past two years, since Dan and I got involved in the home and school association, we've had added work to do. We questioned at the beginning whether or not we had the resources or the time to take on this involvement, but we felt strongly that it was a social obligation, as well as a practical help for our children. So we couldn't say no.

At first, we both attended all the meetings, of both schools involved, so that we could get to know them together, since they are so different from one another. Then we divided our labors. Dan went to Michael's school and I went to Frank's.

It's very demanding, and at least for now, no results are evident. I won't hide the fact that more than once Dan and I were on the verge of giving up. It all seemed so useless, and we felt it almost a crime to waste the time because we're always behind on so many things. Still, there is the possibility of establishing new relationships, of stimulating renewed vigor, of getting things moving, and of being, at least to some extent, in touch with the problems of today. So we'll try to persevere. We can't worry about immediate results. We'll have to look at the long-range effects.

Today while returning from the meeting, I was talking with the mother of one of Frank's friends. She and her husband are people of humble origins. She told me about her life and the difficulties of adjustment that her son was going through at school. I shared with her other kinds of problems. We examined how we could help one another, and others too.

The death of grandfather

May 21, 1975

Dad is rapidly declining, I had not seen him for a week. Everything in him is fading; every faculty, every ability, his very awareness is approaching death.

It's striking to see a man as intelligent as Dad is, often unable to put his thoughts together, nor even his words. His eyes are closed. His voice is a garbled noise when it doesn't fade altogether. His legs no longer support him. His hands shake.

Sickness. Death. It's really the extreme disunity of one's body, of one's being. It's consummation.

"It's hard for me to recognize you," he had said to some of us—his children. "I get you mixed up." "Sometimes I'm delirious. I go out of my head."

What a thing it is to see a man face to face with death, in agony! It's as if Dad is on the ridge of a mountain, between life and the beyond. And sometimes he's aware of his condition: "Look what I'm reduced to!"

I can see that *everything* in him is dying and that he has lived his whole life to arrive at this point.

"How's it going, Dad?"

He looks at me. "As God wants."

He's now fully aware of what he's saying.

"I'm not going to complain."

You can feel he's accepting his death.

As he receives Communion, he says, "The body of Christ!" I understood that we are really all "body of Christ," and that I wasn't just with my Dad, but with someone who forms part of the "body" of Jesus.

May 22, 1975

Dad is less and less conscious; but he still has moments of lucidity in which he suffers from his condition. But he doesn't rebel. He accepts it.

I took him from one room to another in a wheelchair. His eyes are at times blank. At times he says things that make sense, at times nonsense. It's painful to watch.

But if we're all one body in Jesus, I can share in the life, and above all in the death, of my Dad.

That's what these days are supposed to be all about. To die with Dad. In this way I can, in every moment, offer not so much my own sorrows, but mainly the sorrows of Dad, for whom I am living these days.

For Pentecost, the Holy Father gave a beautiful "Apostolic Exhortation" on joy.

We read it here in the house, and it strengthened the atmosphere that has been created in these days. It's an atmosphere of deep serenity; one of joy. There is still laughter, at times. There's some joking. But it's not an attempt at distraction; it's not an attempt to avoid suffering.

May 25, 1975

These days have been very special. We are very much in the truth. We're living in touch with death and helping one another not to be afraid of it. It's a reality of life. It's a momentous reality of the Christian life. It is the sublimation of the human being. It is complete fulfillment.

Those watching from a distance (many friends come to visit and look on apprehensively) say, "What a shame!"

They don't understand. Yet maybe after they stay here a while, they begin to realize that here there's a different way of looking at life.

We live the present moment. We try to adhere to the "new" reality of every moment. When you're next to a sick person, there's something new all the time.

There are especially precious moments in each day; for example, when I am alone with Dad. He's now in a state of total mental disorganization. Yet, by helping him, by suffering with him, by carrying on the interminable conversations unrelated to time or space, all this nourishes the relationship with him and makes it at times even deeper than before.

It's a relationship with a man who seems to be saying with his whole being, "Why?" It's a little like Jesus on the cross who cried out, "My God, my God, why have you forsaken me?"

There are also some beautiful moments spent with

Mom, or with my brothers or with other relatives who come to stay with Dad. Life becomes simple. What stands out is the truth, the essential, what is of worth in our relationship with each other. Dad is now out of touch, but we act as if he were fully conscious. We take him into account in our conversations, in our silence, in our actions.

Some others who come, though they have every good intention, make me feel ashamed, as if I were being offensive toward Dad and was lacking in respect for him. They feel pity and compassion for him, but they speak and act in his presence as if he were already dead.

May 26, 1975

It's a deprivation. It's a real severing, this slow but irreversible and constantly new loss of Dad.

It's as if something in me is dying with him. A relationship is dying. A mutual understanding is dying. A security deriving from love is dying. In a certain way, the "roots" of my human life are dying. If he hadn't been there, I would not have had the gift of life. And he is dying. I will remain to carry on his function in the world. It's as if he were passing on the responsibility to me. He fought the battle. He's arrived at the goal. And I will continue the race.

From person to person, from death to death, humanity moves on toward the finish line.

But this sense of death that I have from being with my dying father is not only due to the fact that it's my father who's dying, the man who gave me life. It's there also, and especially, because a Christian is dying, a "brother," one with whom I have had a deep understanding that goes beyond our limitations, our personalities, our human conditioning.

There is a bond that's stronger than all else, a "blood relationship." The blood that links us is the blood of Christ.

This detachment of person from person, and especially of Christian from Christian, is a legitimate suffering because we were created to be "body of Christ," and we feel as if parts of that body are being torn from each other when we have to be separated in time and space.

But *this* is the moment of faith. *This* is the moment of love.

Faith in these moments is like a lens. Without a lens, everything is dark, out of focus, doubtful, uncertain, obscure. With a lens, all is clear, luminous, vibrant, sure.... Everything is alive.... Death is life.

This is the moment of love. I understand that the greatest act of love of a person is death—to say with *all one's being*, "I am nothing; You are everything."

May 28, 1975

I have to let myself be pruned....

"Jesus, prune away in me all that is not you."

Some of the shoots that the Father prunes, are dead, but others are alive. And the sap flows from the live cut.

Our prunings are of the live variety. And they hurt. Blood and water flow from them—something both divine and human, that is.

I don't find consolation from the thought that in a

short while Dad will be in the other life and will no longer suffer.

I realize that every moment, every breath, every suffering of his and ours has a value, has an impact both in time and in eternity. So I don't desire that this suffering, this thrust, end prematurely.

What consoled me instead is the effort to live moment by moment the expected and the unexpected with decisiveness and in depth. Eternal life begins right here.

Based on what seems to be logical reasoning, many people are in favor of euthanasia. Without God, without Jesus, humankind has no outlet, and human life—even though everyone seems to be struggling to make something of it—is deprived of that "infinite" value that it takes on by participation in the divine life for which man is destined.

Why prolong Dad's suffering by continuing to care for him as well as possible? Why prolong Mom's agony when we know that our efforts will come to nothing in the face of an illness of this kind?

The reason: God is the ruler (the loving ruler) over life and death. Only he knows the moment, the right moment. We put ourselves in his hands with complete trust.

June 6, 1975

Grandpa died in the hospital. He was moved from there to the funeral parlor. My brother and I went alone to see him first. Then my older children arrived.

We all stood there, silent, feeling great sorrow, but containing it.

Later, Dan gathered together our younger children and some of our nieces and nephews—a dozen children in all. Before he brought them in he explained to them: "Now you are going to see Grandpa dead, but what you will see is only the body of Grandpa because his soul is already in heaven with Jesus, with the saints. The body you will see will be in a big box; there will be a funeral for him; and then they will take him to the cemetery to bury him. After a short while the body will come apart just as all things do when they decompose. But Jesus said that people will rise again. In a few years from now, when we too will be dead, we'll all be together again in heaven with Grandpa. And at the end of the world our bodies too will share in God's glory. So you don't have to get upset when you see that Grandpa doesn't move anymore, or doesn't talk. Because he's already in heaven where he's waiting to see all of us again. And his body awaits the resurrection. When we're standing in front of Grandpa's body, let's say a prayer. He will hear us. He will see us from heaven and smile. We don't have to worry. It's as if he were in our midst, even though his body isn't moving."

So Dan and the children went before Grandpa's coffin, which was surrounded by lots of flowers. Dan went ahead of them and right away said to them, "Look how peaceful his face is! They say that when the soul leaves the body of a person, it leaves imprinted on the face, the state the person was in in that moment. Look how beautiful he is. It means that his soul was very much at peace. He had prepared for his meeting with Jesus."

We all said a prayer. The children stayed and

looked at Grandpa. They were intent, fully conscious of what was happening. A few tears fell from their eyes, but they weren't mournful. They had this realization that death is a passage and that Grandpa would rise again. What remained in them was a sense of something big, mysterious, that had deep significance—even if hidden.

We had the funeral, and when we accompanied the body to the cemetery, the children all wanted to be around the coffin. They were serene. They were alert to the situation. What they were taking part in was a rite, a ceremony that had meaning for them. That body was something precious.

Glimpses of life with the children

Clare

About two years ago, while Dan was attempting to put a beautiful country church on canvas, Clare and I took a walk down a little road that ran through a meadow. At first we spoke little, but I could tell Clare had something on her mind.

"Mom, I think I've really understood what my vocation is."

I felt a lump in my throat.

"Wonderful, Clare. I'm happy for you!"

She pulled a copy of a letter out of her jacket pocket. In it she had described, with great simplicity and depth, her life during that period and her decision to give her life completely to God.

Some time ago, when she was about fifteen, a guest

was questioning her and she responded more or less in these words:

"We were born into an atmosphere in which the only way of life for us was to care about one another and to care about everyone else.

"At one time, I thought that the whole world was like this; that everyone tried to live in this way. Then, after going to school and getting to know other people, I saw that things weren't like that. There was overwhelming suffering, deep loneliness, injustice, indifference. I then understood that the Gospel entailed a choice that meant going against the current.

"I felt that up until then, I had been living on a kind of grant; on the love between Mom and Dad and among us all—as if this were normal. Now I had to decide what I wanted. I could live the life that all the others did, or. . . . I was in this state for a few months. I didn't make a choice. And my life felt empty. Then I decided to live as a Christian for the rest of my life. Now I can see how much my family had helped me— without the least bit of intimidation. No one had told me in that period what I 'had' to do."

September 16, 1978

Here's something Dan wrote down:

"This evening, I gave my blessing to Clare and then I gave her a kiss. She's leaving tomorrow for Loppiano* and she'll enter the Focolare.** It's her way. We

---

*A small town of the Focolare Movement near Florence where several hundred young people coming from all over the world are formed according to a deep experience of Christian life.

**Community of lay persons completely consecrated to the evangelical ideal of unity in mutual love. It gave rise to the above-mentioned Movement.

68

feel that's evident. She's happy. So this gives a deep joy to Anne and me too. Our oldest girl, consecrated to God.... We had written on her birth announcement: 'May her life be resplendent for the glory of the Lord.'

"In these past few days, Clare has been packing her bags together with Anne, in an orderly and serene manner. Yesterday we packed her 'valuables,' just a few things. A little golden necklace and bracelet. We handed over her savings from her recent earnings.

"The Lord asks our detachment also from our children. One at a time. Only the love that we have had for them remains."

September 17, 1978

Another something that Dan wrote down....

"Well, Clare's gone. We had dinner together as a parting celebration for her. Only Frank was missing. In the afternoon, Mike took her to the car that would take her to Loppiano. I wanted to say something special to her, but it wasn't possible with the children present.

"This evening she's no longer with us. Along with the happiness we feel over Clare's choice, we both have some sorrow. We thought of Mary who gave Jesus, her child, for the others, for all of us. We feel a little like her. But we can't dwell on our 'loss.' We have to go ahead and continue to live...."

December 29, 1978

It's already two months since Clare left. We feel her absence. During the last two years she was often away because of many commitments, but we always felt her presence just the same. Even with her active and demanding lifestyle, she conveyed a sense of peace, of serenity, of simplicity. We no longer hear her laughter, her words; nor is there her silence, which was always constructive. But we're happy for her.

Today we received a letter from her. She had a special message for each of us. She asked us to look after a school friend of hers. She told us a little about her life now: "I'm very happy here. Everything has changed, and yet nothing has changed. The Ideal for which I live is always that one we know, and yet it's always new, to be lived better.... There's always something new— fairly frequent changes. That's very good, because it prevents us from becoming accustomed to and dependent on a certain way of life, or from becoming too attached to things and people.... Also, you find that there's always a new and greater gift of God awaiting you...."

Maryann

December, 1976

Some time ago, one of Maryann's friends interviewed her for a magazine. After describing a visit to her studio, and the welcome Maryann gave her, she presents, in Maryann's own words, her experience at art school:

"There were people of every kind, with all manner of ideas, at the school. Many of them took drugs regularly. At first, I thought it was impossible to establish a friendship with anyone, but I felt I had to try. I had to show concern for everyone I met. For example, the first thing I decided to do was to learn the names of everyone I met. Then when I would see them again, I would say their names, as if we had known one another for a while. I made friendships with those who seemed most alone, such as with a boy whose face was badly marked with scars. He would beam every time I went out of my way to say hello to him. One day a boy I knew to be addicted to drugs offered me a ride home in his car because he was heading in my direction. I said okay, even though I felt a little uneasy. I wanted to make him feel that he could gain someone's trust and friendship. Strangely enough, my fears disappeared and I felt everything would work out. When we arrived at the car, we found that he was hopelessly blocked in. We parted cordially, and in his eyes I could sense a feeling of gratitude. It's the same thing, whether I'm going to an exhibition or going out for pizza—I try always to be so disposed toward the others. I have seen that a simple and sincere relationship with people results. 'Even though our ideas are different,' a friend of mine told me on the bus, 'it feels very good to be together with you. I don't know why.' Also, one morning during one of our drawing classes while I was intent on my work, the professor came up to me and asked if I believed in God. I was almost dumbfounded, and I told him yes, adding cautiously, 'Why?' And he answered very simply, 'Because I can tell.'"

"What about Nancy, that girl you once spoke about? How is she?"

"Oh yes, Nancy.... One day while our anatomy teacher was projecting a slide of a human fetus on the screen, she asked me, almost certain I would be in agreement, 'Can anybody possibly believe that little, ugly thing could be a human being?' I answered her that

71

she too started out like that. At that moment I felt that I had caused a division between us and that she would probably not talk to me anymore. But instead we became good friends. We would often spend time together and it would be she who suggested it. Just a few days ago, she got the urge for the first time to open up to me. She admitted, with some embarrassment, to the squalor of some of her experiences, and to the need for acting with greater integrity towards others and towards herself. So you see, what seemingly unites me to my companions is art, but I feel that my relationship with anyone is a true one and grows, only to the extent that I can show them love."

Maryann said these last words very matter-of-factly, but one could see they expressed her life, the essence of her daily experience.

Michael

I found a crumpled up copy of a piece done by Michael, when he was fifteen, for a little publication made for children.

"My life always had a Christian basis to it—ever since I was born, I could say. This has contributed greatly to our upbringing. Together we had to try constantly to build the family, by being united in the face of everyday problems, by sharing all sufferings, by communicating with one another about our things.

"Naturally, it hasn't always been easy. There have been critical moments that have shaken everybody up a little. In these times there has always been a certain tendency in each of us to look for a resolution to the difficulty, to continue to go ahead and not let things get us down.

"For example one thing that hurt me was the lack of a deep relationship between Dad and myself during a particular period of my life. This stemmed partly from the differences in our personalities, partly from the fact that we're both rather reserved people and it was partly due to a certain 'reverence' (which was not all that balanced) which I had toward him.

"Just a few days ago, at a time in which I needed to make some important choices. I found the opportunity (with the encouragement of my mother and sister) of speaking with him. From that half hour chat there developed a relationship that not only helped me make my choice, but made me understand the mistaken judgments I had formed about Dad.

"With Mom, I have always had a beautiful relationship. We always felt free to talk to one another about anything. Quite often, Mom talks to us about her problems or asks our opinion about something relating to one or another of us.

"On the other hand, all the problems that concern the whole family (the budget, things to buy, things to do) get discussed every so often, so that we can assess them in relation to the ideal of our life."

Questions asked of Michael during a meeting of families.

Question: "What brought you to live this way?" (They were talking about his Christian experience.)

Michael: "In my adolescent years, I was faced with the reality of a world around me that attracted me because I saw certain values in it, or what seemed to be values. Still, I don't know why, all this had a somewhat dampening effect on that Christian life that my family passed on to me—more with deeds than with words.

"At a certain point, I found I had to make a choice. I went through two rather difficult years in which I was struggling with very serious questions. In the end I saw clearly that the things offered to me by society didn't give me that trust, that joy, that peace I had found in trying to live the Gospel in every moment.

"Dad and Mom were looking on, without pushing me in one direction or another. But their presence was undoubtedly a determining factor. They were a fixed reference point that became for me a verification and prevented me from being dragged along by feelings and impulses."

Question: "How do you live this life at school?"

Michael: "In a very simple way. Friendships have been growing in my class over the past years. A few of us get together often to exchange ideas, discuss problems, etc. In addition, we've been working together to carry out (within the limits of our capabilities) a series of activities that benefit the elderly, the lonely, or just people with some sort of need.

"Then there is the main body of students.

"In the more restricted gatherings, where I'm able to establish more personal associations, I try—drawing from my somewhat limited background—to make a contribution toward a peaceful and well thought-out solution to the various problems dealt with.

"When there are large assemblies (seven to eight hundred persons), and the element of mass suggestion is such that you can't give anything that will really be properly received, then the only thing to do is first to "suffer" in the face of certain ideas that are radically in error. Then if it's the case, I also try to say something in order to help deal with concrete and very difficult situations in which we students often find ourselves.

"I feel this kind of involvement is very important in order to show that a Christian is one who is authentically committed in life, a person who is immersed in society and not withdrawn from it."

March 17, 1977

Today, listening to one of those phone-in radio programs on which they were talking about the relationship between parents and children, and during which some mothers and fathers had called in, Michael called in too. He had a tape recorder handy so his conversation was recorded and I was able to get a transcript of it.

Question: "Hello, Michael? What's on your mind? Why did you call in?"

Michael: "I wanted to call after I heard the story of that woman whose sixteen-year-old boy was seriously harmed by drugs. When I heard that the boy's father was rarely at home because he was out trying to make a lot of money so he could give his son more, I ended up comparing this situation to mine. You see, in my case, from the time I was very small, I was always used to having both parents around regularly, not just one. And they never had any qualms about putting their relationship with us children and our upbringing ahead of their own possible gain or their own careers.

"From the time we were little, we had the figure of our father before us, not in the sense that he was home

75

all day, but because his 'presence' was always strongly felt due to his example and his love.

"For example, when we were still small, in the evenings he would tell us stories, various episodes, or things about his life, very simple things.

"When we got a little older, he was a lot of help to us at those times in which one or another of us would have to make some important choice. He would always get us to reason things out without ever being domineering, without ever imposing himself."

Question: "Can you tell us an instance in which you found support from your father?"

Michael: "When I was fourteen or fifteen, like everyone else, I came up against problems related to sex. I met some girls...the usual story. And I saw how, being aware of my situation and also my mistakes, my father could conduct himself in such a way that I would want to tell him what was happening to me. Then, like two friends, we would examine together what was going on inside me. And together we would try to do something about it in a calm, rational manner, trying to avoid any harsh reactions in me.

"Only recently, I asked Dad how he had been able to bring this off, because I have seen that many of my friends have never been able to talk with their parents. He answered that although his professional training could have enabled him to make a lot of money and eventually leave us with material wealth, he had passed up this opportunity so he could be closer to us at the start of our lives during our infancy and adolescence, so that we'd be really capable of building a life for ourselves. This is because he didn't consider us his private property, someone he could ignore or impose upon as he wished.

"All this was always done in close collaboration with Mom. She too was always present. In fact, maybe we boys could open up even more easily with her. I think it's just natural.

"My sisters are older than I am. One is twenty-three and the other twenty-two. They're still living at home although the older one who is about to get her master's will probably be leaving soon. Her presence has been very important in our relationship with our parents, because she's a very complete person and she's contributed a lot to the workings of the family."

Question: "With these parents of yours, father and mother together, have you had any positive experiences with respect to authority—which can also mean protection?"

Michael: "Yes. Often. At times they leave us free to decide certain things, though they make clear to us the difficulties involved and the dangers we can run up against. At times they lay down the law a little, maybe not allowing us to go somewhere or do something."

Question: "So in this upbringing, you've also heard the word, 'no.' "

Michael: "Of course."

Question: "And how have you handled this 'no'?"

Michael: "Sometimes well and sometimes not so well. I'd like you to show me the person who could always take it well. But maybe after some time passed by—maybe even a year or so—we've seen that the 'no' was right."

Question: "And probably that 'no' was more palatable because your mother and father backed it up with an integrity of life."

Michael: "Precisely. This we could always sense, so it certainly helped us to better accept what they would say to us."

Interviewer: "Thank you very much, Michael, for your story. It's probably the first we've heard on this program that was so positive. We're accustomed to more negative experiences. So long and thanks again."

December 30, 1978

When Michael saw that I was putting these notes together, he wrote the following:

"Very often, people say that our family is special. We're free, distinct, and deeply united—all at the same time. Each of us children goes along his or her own path, sometimes far from home; yet at the same time we remain anchored to a concept of the family that some might call traditional, and, what is more important, to a kind of family life that is no longer very common.

"To tell you the truth, only this year have I myself come to recognize this. John has moved away because of his job; Clare has set sail for new shores; Maryann is away at school; Frank is still at home; and I live in town with some students. We get home only occasionally, and then only for short stays.

"It's true that at some time or another every family has to separate so that each member can find his or her own way in life. But with us, this came a little unexpectedly and wasn't immediately planned for. Circumstances were such that we had to be divided. At first, perhaps because we've been used to a certain flexibility

78

in our affairs, it didn't have too unsettling an effect on us. But after a few weeks of physical separation, I began to miss our life together at home. Before, I was never alone for more than a few days. Now it's sometimes months. I've come to realize what a treasure our family life is, and that is, in great part, a credit to my parents, who have given us this heritage. It will enable us, whether we live alone or with others, to use that touch of imagination that will create 'family' no matter where we go. We've received the universal dimension of the family that can be brought to bear on every particular situation.

"It's often said that the concept of the family as the basic unit of society is being seriously questioned. And this is understandable with respect to certain types of family. But it's not at all applicable to the sort of family in which there's a sense of service, of availability; where there's the effort to adjust one's own needs to those of the others; where there is the most complete openness.

"To survive, a family has to build something special through its relationships, its conversation, its mutual enrichment, its deep intimacy and then be guided beyond its confines by those same elements that have made it what it is. I think my family has accomplished this and is still doing so. This is the heritage I have received from it—a social dimension in our dwelling together that really builds society."

John

Once John was asked to speak before a group of people about his life. I found some notes that he made for that event.

"I went to a high school that bordered on a very rough area of the city and some of the students came from there. Many of them had been through the most sordid experiences.

"The first year was terrible. I isolated myself from everyone. I didn't know what I was going to do. Then I met a boy who, like me, wanted to live as a Christian. So we made an agreement to be as united as possible so we could maybe do something even about an environment such as ours. Together we thrust ourselves into the situation, trying to understand, to make friendships, especially with those students who were the most lonely, the poorest, or had the most serious problems. A whole new life emerged for us.

"Across from our school there is an institution for the handicapped. We felt the desire to go there and get to know them. We helped them with their work. We tried to make them feel less alone and unusual. Every chance we got, we went there. Some other students from our school began to go with us.

"My high school years became filled with rich and beautiful experiences for me, especially the last two years.

"After graduation, I worked for a time in a large firm as a draftsman. I was working mostly with middle-aged people, and their problems were in a certain respect much more serious than those I had come up against in high school. There was a great deal of apathy and more immorality than I had ever encountered. And I was alone there. At times I felt I was smothering under the pall of mediocrity and vulgarity. I was alone. But I did have someone to help me: Jesus in the Eucharist.

"At first I got to know the younger people there; then others. Little by little a few of them told me something about their lives, and I began to understand that beneath all that squalor there were many troubles.

"I don't work there any more, but I've returned a number of times to say hello to various friends. And it's always been a special treat for me, and for them too, as they've indicated."

May 15, 1978

This evening John moved out. He's in a workstudy program in another town. We went to the station to say good-bye. Dan took some pictures before we left.

Our John.... Just nineteen years old and he's off to another city where the style of life isn't always the best.

We can trust John, with his moral stature, his simplicity, his capacity to make friends without being too influenced by them in certain areas. But it's natural that underneath it all we're a little apprehensive.

May 18, 1978

John called us long distance. He seems okay now. His first day on the job was a little rougher than he thought it would be. But today he ran into two young people whom he had met at a large gathering a while ago. He had lunch with them and it lifted his spirits a bit. They talked about many things of mutual interest to them and he felt less alone.

May 20, 1978

Today Frank got a card from John. It got passed

around so much that I can't find it anymore, but it went something like this: "Greetings from my apartment. I've got my difficulties, but no one's stopping me from loving all those I meet. I'm really doing well. Good-bye for now. John."

May 28, 1978

Dan wrote to John today. We feel we should keep in close touch as much as possible, especially during this initial period—even though we're sure that this time away, getting to know new people and situations, will be good for him.

Dan wrote the following:

"Dear John, we thought we'd write you about the latest news. First of of all, how are you? We read your post card to Frank in which you mentioned having some difficulties. You can be sure that we're with you in these things. We think of you often, especially when we're together in the evening.

"The other day, the washing machine broke down. Our first impulse was to say, 'Get John.' Fortunately Charlie from next door came over to fix it. Otherwise who knows when it would have been repaired?

"Our days are always filled. I took part in a very important two-day meeting with some people who are involved in the social and religious field. It was a very powerful experience for me. I saw once again what a great gift God has given us in making us Christians, with the possibility of renewing ourselves continuously and becoming 'new'. So even if the world is going the way it's going (and I'm sure you see enough of that) there is a hope that is stronger than the evil that exists. This hope comes from God.

"Yesterday, I met some friends of yours at a gathering for artists—Paul, Mike, Charlie, Joe and others—all great artists, I'm sure!

"Your mother is working hard as usual, with the help of Clare, our speed typist. She didn't go to the gathering for artists. (As you know, she doesn't consider herself much of an artist.) Actually it would do her a lot of good to get away from her work to hear some of the music and see some of the pantomines, etc.

"Yesterday, Frank brought home a kitten, just two or three weeks old. Your mother had her first encounter with it when she returned home late yesterday evening and opened the bathroom door. You can imagine her great joy....

"Maryann took its picture with your camera and right now she's working on developing the film. I have my doubts.... I don't think you've taught her the art well enough yet.

"Maryann got an offer to illustrate a children's book based on the *Divine Comedy*—little money but a lot of recognition. She took the job.

"So, John. That's the news. Remember Margaret? She's back in the hospital. She's dying. We went to see her. She's at peace, in the certainty of God's love.

"Keep us in mind, John. You're always with us. All our love. Dad."

June 20, 1978

John stopped in for a few hours today. He was on his way to another city where the company wants him to work for a while. He seems pretty happy, even if he's a little disillusioned and a little concerned about the new place he's being moved to for the next few months.

83

We spoke about a lot of things. He also had us laughing till our sides split when he told us how he was fending for himself in his own apartment. He brought some pictures, too.

Amidst the laughter there was serious talk, too—especially about the indifference and the spiritual and physical inactivity of the environment in which he found himself.

July 26, 1978

We've been on vacation for a few days now. We think of John often. We're sure that in the summer months, he'll find it even harder to be away. Dan wrote him this letter:

"We're sorry that you're there working while we're here vacationing, but you are in our thoughts. I can well imagine that you'd like to be here. But at least we can tell you by letter to keep up the good fight. We remember you every day, John, when we receive Jesus in the Eucharist. We, too, are committed to a life of going against the current, and even on vacation, the opportunities aren't lacking.

"Your mother, Frank and Grandmother all send a special hello. All the others are at different Mariapolis gatherings.

"We visited my father on the way. He's doing well. He told us old war stories, and how he met my mother. It all seems so long ago, yet all of us came from their love.

"The weather has been nice here, so we've taken a few trips around. I did some painting again. There are some nice views from Grandma's house. There's a lovely church off in the distance, and this is a reminder to greet Jesus and to live the present moment well.

"The day before yesterday, I encountered your friend, Henry, whom you met here last year.

"The countryside is beautiful, just as you must remember it. I'll say so long for now, John. A big hello from everyone here. Dad."

July 30, 1978

We got a fast reply from John:

"Dear everybody, I just received Dad's letter and I was really happy to hear you're all doing so well.

"I'm doing well, too, despite the sometimes dampening effects of some of the life around me. But things are improving with time. Some real good friend-ships are developing and people at least smile when I say hello to them.

"I am going through a very powerful experience. It involves that relationship with God which perhaps before I didn't understand too well. When I was home, I went to Mass every day; I had a very active life, a solidly united family behind me which protected me. But even this situation could have become a comfortable routine.

"Then all at once, a lot of this was gone and was replaced by other things: new acquaintances, new places, different mentalities, the excitement of writing home and telling everyone about my experiences, etc. Then the novelty wore off and all the joys of my new situation suddenly seemed to fade away. Then...a sense of emptiness. But precisely in such moments, the figure of Jesus stands out in all his fulness and he fills every emptiness.

"Then you no longer think of what's coming, but of the moment that you are in, which is swiftly passing by. You realize that your moments of loneliness can best be filled by prayers for your fellow employees, those perhaps who are farthest from God.

"I always carry with me a card that says, 'Make of every obstacle a springboard.' It's really perfect for my situation.

"I often go to the beach to swim and get some sun.

"Some new people have been hired. They were hired about a month after me. Like it or not, looking at them, I can't help feeling a degree of accomplishment at having been on the job for a while.

"A few friends are being transferred to another location, so I'll miss them.

"Well, I hope I can come to visit you soon, but I'm sure I can't get off for more than a few days. Say hello to everyone for me, especially Mom and Grandma. Have a great vacation! John."

Frank

March 10, 1977

This is what Frank had to say:

"For some time, now, I've felt the need to go to Mass every day. I decided to go in the morning before classes began.

"One day, some of my friends saw me go into church and they began to kid me. What hurt was not so much the kidding (this I could take without any trouble) but the fact that they relegated me to the category of a person who went to Mass just out of habit, like a machine. Instead, I consciously decide what I want to do, and I do what I'm convinced of.

"This went on for a week. Then they stopped it. The situation changed. They now let me exercise my faith, and for my part, I try to look for those things that unite us, not the things that divide us.

"Now we have mutual respect for one another, and this respect is turning into real friendship with some of them."

September 23, 1977

Yesterday evening, Frank went to have supper at the home of a friend who was celebrating his birthday. Eleven o'clock came and he still wasn't home, so we began to worry—especially because he had his motor bike and had a good stretch of highway to travel. Dan, who was more upset than I was, phoned a friend whose son was also at the party.

"Don't worry," he said to Dan, "around here (we had just moved to a new area) they stay up later."

At midnight, Frank was still out.

Dan, who was terribly upset, finally found the phone number of Frank's friend. He asked for Frank and in the coolest tone of voice, he told him to return home immediately.

Only a few minutes later, Frank came in. (Who knows if he even had a chance to say good-bye to his friends in the rush to leave.) His father's tone of voice, so unlike the usual one, must have struck him deeply. Dan was there to greet him at the door, still rather upset.

The next morning, as soon as he awakened, Dan

said to me, "You'd better get our little stray up."

I sat down at the foot of Frank's bed. Still half a-sleep, he was trying hard to open his eyes so he could get up and go to school. I kidded him a little, and half joking, half serious, I reminded him of last night's drama, with all its episodes, also referring to how upset I was and especially how upset Dan was.

In a tone of disappointment, but without a trace of anger over our stern actions, Frank told me something about the party. In the end, he admitted that he wasn't very impressed by this nocturnal event. In fact, he concluded by saying, "You know, it wasn't the least bit fun."

January 15, 1978

I set down my shopping bags in the kitchen and then walked past the bathroom. On the sink were some swabs of blood-soaked cotton and some peroxide. There was dirt all over. "What happened?" I thought.

I found out Frank had taken a spill on his way to school, when his motor bike skidded on the curve at the bottom of the hill. The night had been very cold and the street was still icy. He didn't hurt himself badly; it could have been worse.

Oh, that motor bike! How much I think about it when Frank is late. He has to ride on very busy streets, and sometimes they're wet or icy. They're so dangerous.

A friend of mine said just the other day, "I would never give my children permission to go around on those 'death traps.' I don't know how you can stand it, knowing your boy is always in danger!"

She made me think. When we moved to this area a few months ago, this problem came up. Frank has to go three or four miles to school, and just as far for basket-ball practice. The same thing for visiting his friends. They're all a good distance away. Then he has to go to the library to do his "research." And so on. He would be on the bus all day—or otherwise be walking awfully long distances.

It was hard enough for him to move away from our old neighborhood, leaving his friends, the big-city bustle, his rowing, etc., etc. With all that, we didn't feel we could deny him this motor bike, even if his brothers kidded him and preached to him a little about it. "Well look at that! How do you rate? You must think you're an only child! When we were your age we didn't dare speak of a tricycle much less a motor bike!"

Amidst all the joking, the conversation got serious. "Well, is money the problem?" Frank had said.

"Not so much—or not only."

"Well then, it's because you're afraid I'll hurt myself. So in order not to have to worry yourself about me, you'd rather I didn't get one. Well, you can't put restrictions on my life just so you won't have to worry!"

"You're right, Frank. But we're worried because we care for you. On the other hand, this isn't the real problem. We can handle the suffering we feel when we know you're in danger. The thing is that we'd like to feel a certain assurance that you are mature and responsible and that you'd know how to assess the dangers and take proper precautions."

"But I am mature and responsible."

"You are, are you? Well, we hope that's what you'll become."

In the end, the motor bike was purchased.

A few days later, a boy that lives fairly close to us

had a serious accident at a crossroad nearby. Dan took Frank to the site of the accident in order to examine with him the causes and discover what the boy had done wrong. Later, they went to call on the father of the boy.

It all made a strong impression on Frank, and he said he understood more and more that a person has to be careful, especially since many people don't pay attention to the rules of the road.

Facing up to the problem of the dangers our children have to encounter is an everyday thing. Some of them drive a car and are often on the road, often at night. Right from their childhood, we have tried to instill a sense of responsibility in them, toward their own lives and those of others; and we hope that this will now help them to be prudent.

September 10, 1978

A lot of things were going on today. I felt that I was running a long race without a moment's relief.

And there's still a lot more that should get done.

After supper I saw Frank sitting on the sofa, watching TV. He was looking at a western.

I was undecided as to whether I should sit and watch with him for a while or continue doing my work.

I decided to sit down.

We watched together silently. Every so often, I'd exclaim about something, but...there was no sign of life from Frank.

At the end, he stretched out on the sofa, all six-plus feet of him with his long arms and legs, acting exactly his fifteen years of age. He looked at me and said, "Aw...I think I'll go to sleep!" But he didn't budge.

Then, very abruptly: "I really had a bad day today." He then told me about a misunderstanding he had with a friend of his. It made him feel pretty low.

"The fact is, I'm really feeling...well, I don't know how to say it, but it seems that everything is falling apart. All those values that helped me before, that gave meaning to my life, aren't saying anything to me anymore."

"What kind of values?"

"All of them. For example, I go to Mass but don't feel anything. Communion doesn't do a thing for me. And confession...well, the same thing. With people, I'm civil, so to speak—because I'm used to being that way. But even this doesn't make sense to me any longer."

I listened in silence, avoiding the temptation to immediately size up the situation and, much less, the boy. I very simply listened, silencing the preoccupations that came to my mind.

"I don't know what to do.... Maybe I'll begin to better understand these things that bother me so much by talking about them here with you. What do you feel?"

"Well, Frank, I'm not sure myself what to say. I think this may be a special time in your life. I get the impression that up until now you've been carried along by circumstances, by your family situation, by a Christian life that was ready-made for you. And now, maybe the moment has come for you to stand on your own two feet, to consider more deeply the things you do, the decisions you make. Maybe it's time for making certain choices. I think that even in the past, depending on what age and level of maturity you were at, you made

91

your own choices, because you're too independent a type of person just to follow the crowd. Of course, now the choices are more critical."

There was a pause. Then I continued.

"But do you still believe that God exists and loves you?"

"Yes. This I believe. Maybe it's the only thing I still believe in."

"Well then, that's already a lot, an awful lot. Now you have to patiently and slowly try to understand—bringing your intelligence, your will to bear on it—what, for example, confession is, and what all the things which you no longer 'feel' actually are. Our lives have to be guided more and more not by what we feel, but by the will to do what we understand is good."

"That's kind of hard to take. Right now, I just want to do what I like."

"I've noticed. I see how you spare no effort for basketball. You even play when you're sick! The same with your work on your motor bike. You really get into it!"

I said this jokingly, and he laughed.

"You certainly have the will!"

"Yeah! For the things I like!"

"Still, Frank, this is an important period for you. There's no doubt about it: a certain amount of effort on your part is necessary. And I don't think we'll be able to give you much help. It's the moment in which you have to be guided by your choices, not by things and circumstances."

We continued talking for a long time, about all kinds of topics. It was a very peaceful and very uninhibited conversation.

92

I realized that even the rather profound religious upbringing he had received, compared with other young people his age, had to be verified by him at this point in his life. He himself had to be convinced and had to make his choices accordingly.

What does our attitude as parents have to be in these cases?

I don't know. There aren't any hard-and-fast rules. We'll see what to do, moment by moment.

At the End of the Day

February 17, 1979

The day is over. Everyone's in bed.

A worry concerning one of my boys comes to my mind. During the day, my work, my concern for all the others, the many things I have to do, kept this worry from surfacing. Now that I'm alone, it appears again. I can see the possibility of disaster. It's gnawing away at me.

If I analyze things well, I have to say that at the end of almost every day in recent times, I find myself with some sorrow, some sort of worry, with something or other that hurts inside. It might be the illness of one or the other; it might be some difficulty one is having or another's seemingly irresolvable problem.

"But, why?" I find myself asking, "Why is there always some sorrow I have to feel?"

And to whom do I address this "Why?" if not to God, to him who is always there to hear me?

And I understand. If there's any function I have in the family with respect to those who live at my side, it's that of gathering in the joys, the hopes, the beautiful accomplishments... but above all that of absorbing the sorrows, the troubles, the doubts, the "darkness" of every member.

So, today, I listened to one of my boys, and out of everything that he told me, what I took in most was his suffering, his awkwardness over certain situations, his difficulties, the dangers that he faces due to his still young age.

Now, in the late evening, I find all of this within me. That's the way it was yesterday and that's how it will be tomorrow. Circumstances will be different, but there will always be things that hurt.

Yet there is a way out; one that is ever new, always a rediscovery. It's telling Jesus with all my heart, "I welcome this suffering, this thing that I don't want." I welcome it and unite it with his sufferings.

I am so deeply convinced that his torment, his abandonment, has redeemed the world, has redeemed me, has redeemed every one of my children... I'm so convinced of this that I know the only thing to do is to say over and over my "yes." Uniting myself to him, I have to say with my life, "I place myself in your hands, along with these persons who today have made me the gift of their sufferings."